ISBN: 978-1-956159-55-4

© 2024 Stefania Munzi

All rights reserved. Our authors, editors, and designers work hard to develop original, high-quality content. Please respect their efforts and their rights under copyright law.

Do not copy, photocopy, or reproduce this book or any part of this book for use inside or outside the classroom, in commercial or non-commercial settings. It is also forbidden to copy, adapt, or reuse this book or any part of this book for use on websites, blogs, or third-party lesson-sharing websites.

For permission requests or discounts on class sets and bulk orders contact us at:

Alphabet Publishing
29 Milo Drive
Branford, CT 06405 USA
info@alphabetpublishingbooks.com
www.alphabetpublishingbooks.com

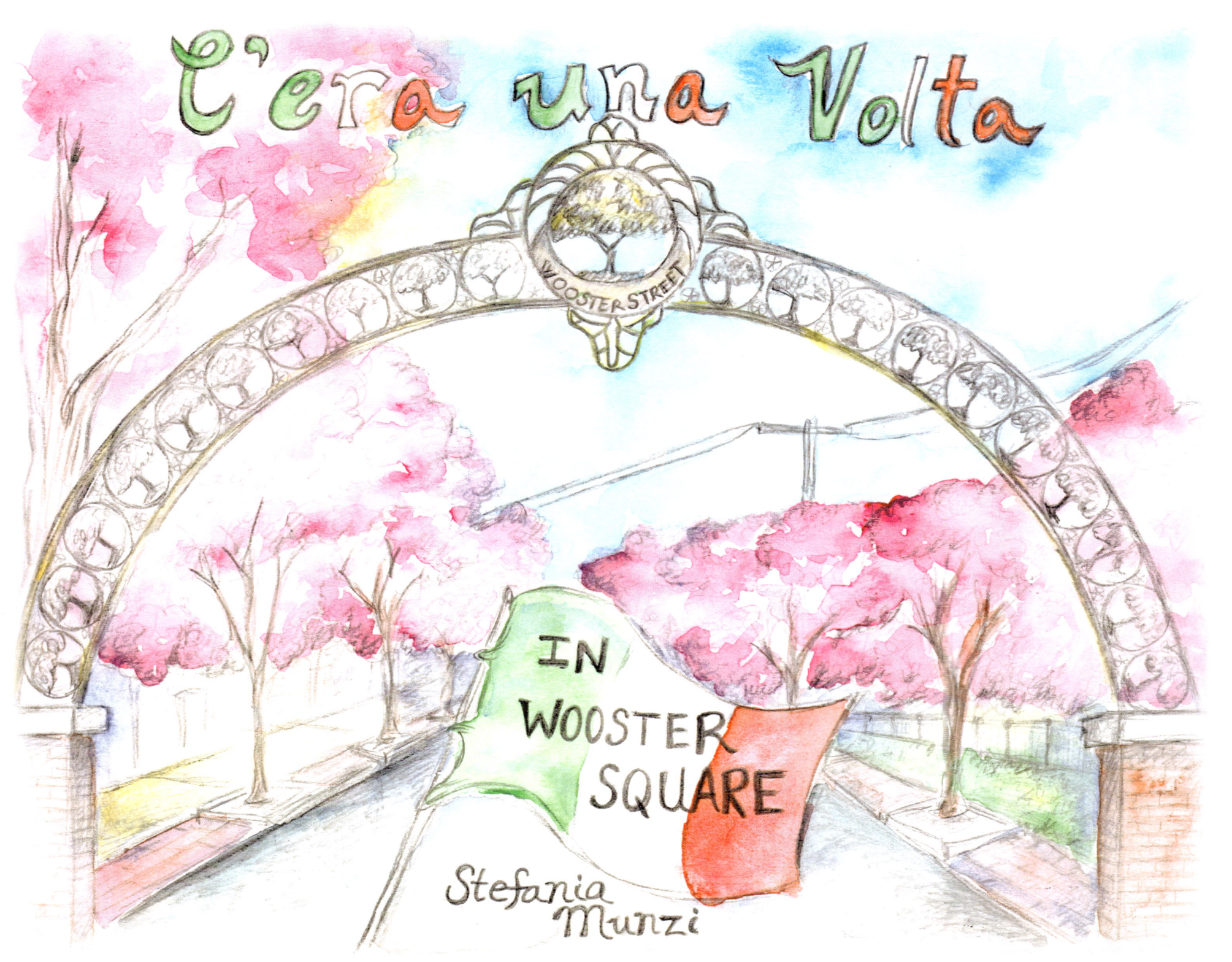

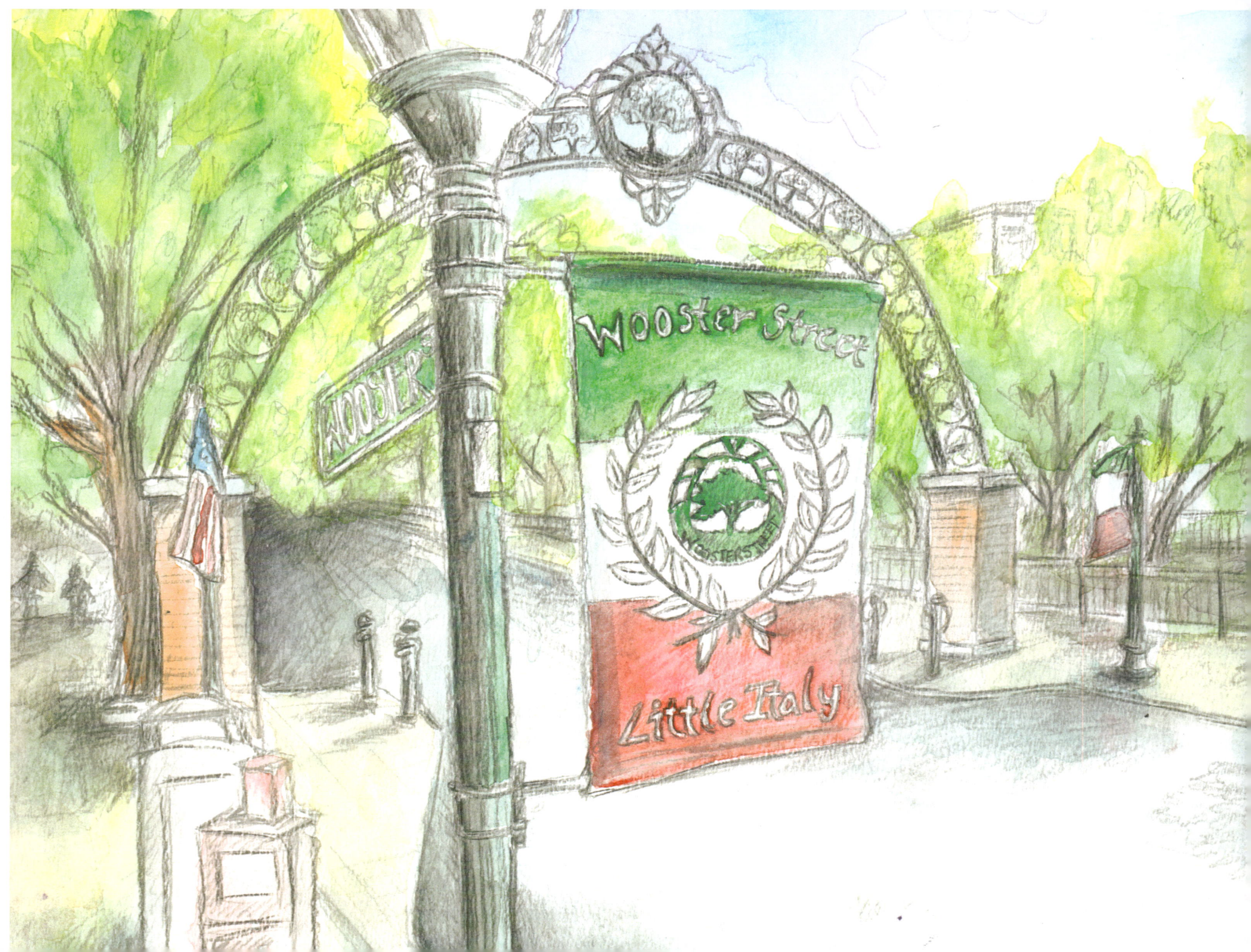

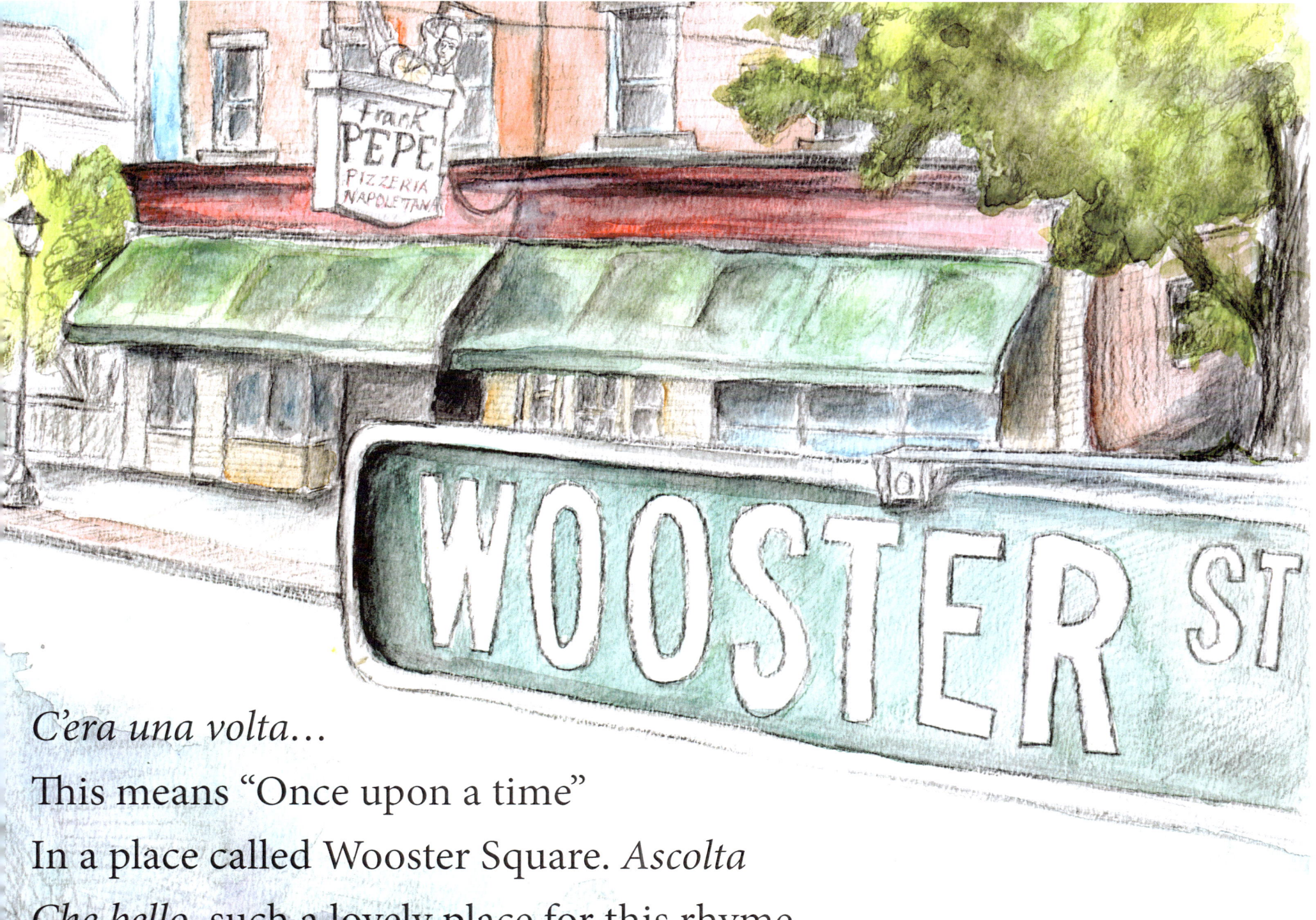

C'era una volta...
This means "Once upon a time"
In a place called Wooster Square. *Ascolta*
Che bello, such a lovely place for this rhyme.

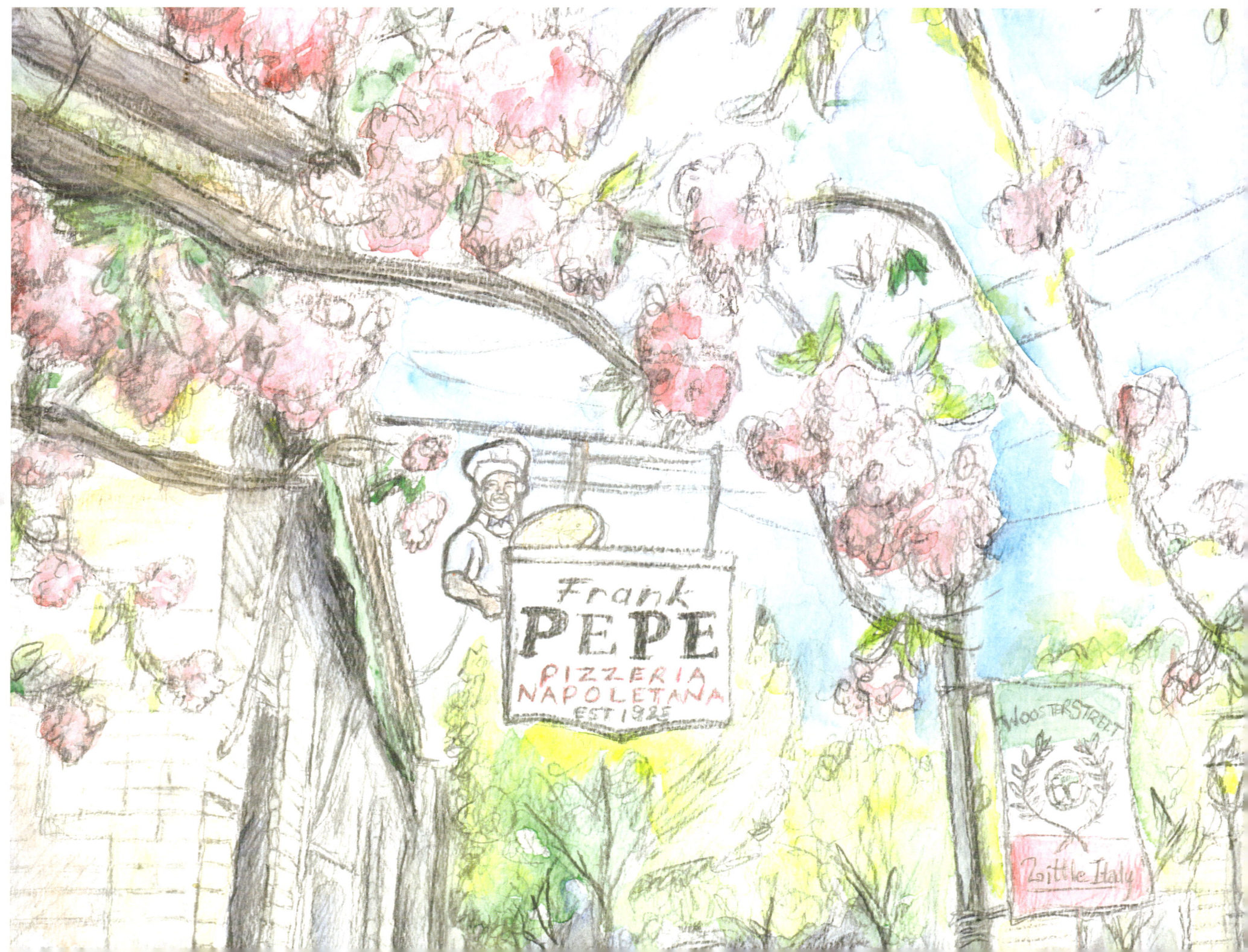

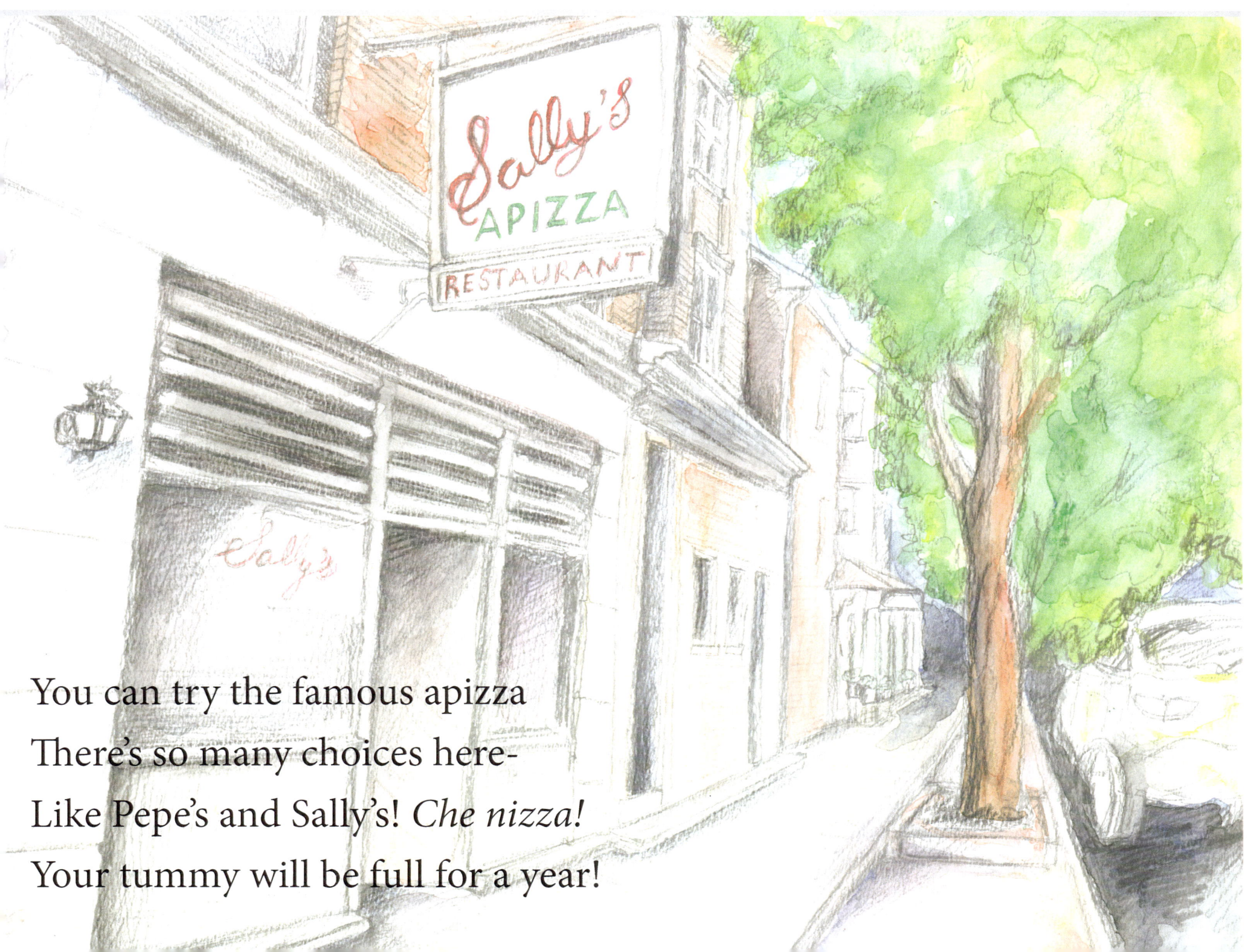

You can try the famous apizza
There's so many choices here—
Like Pepe's and Sally's! *Che nizza!*
Your tummy will be full for a year!

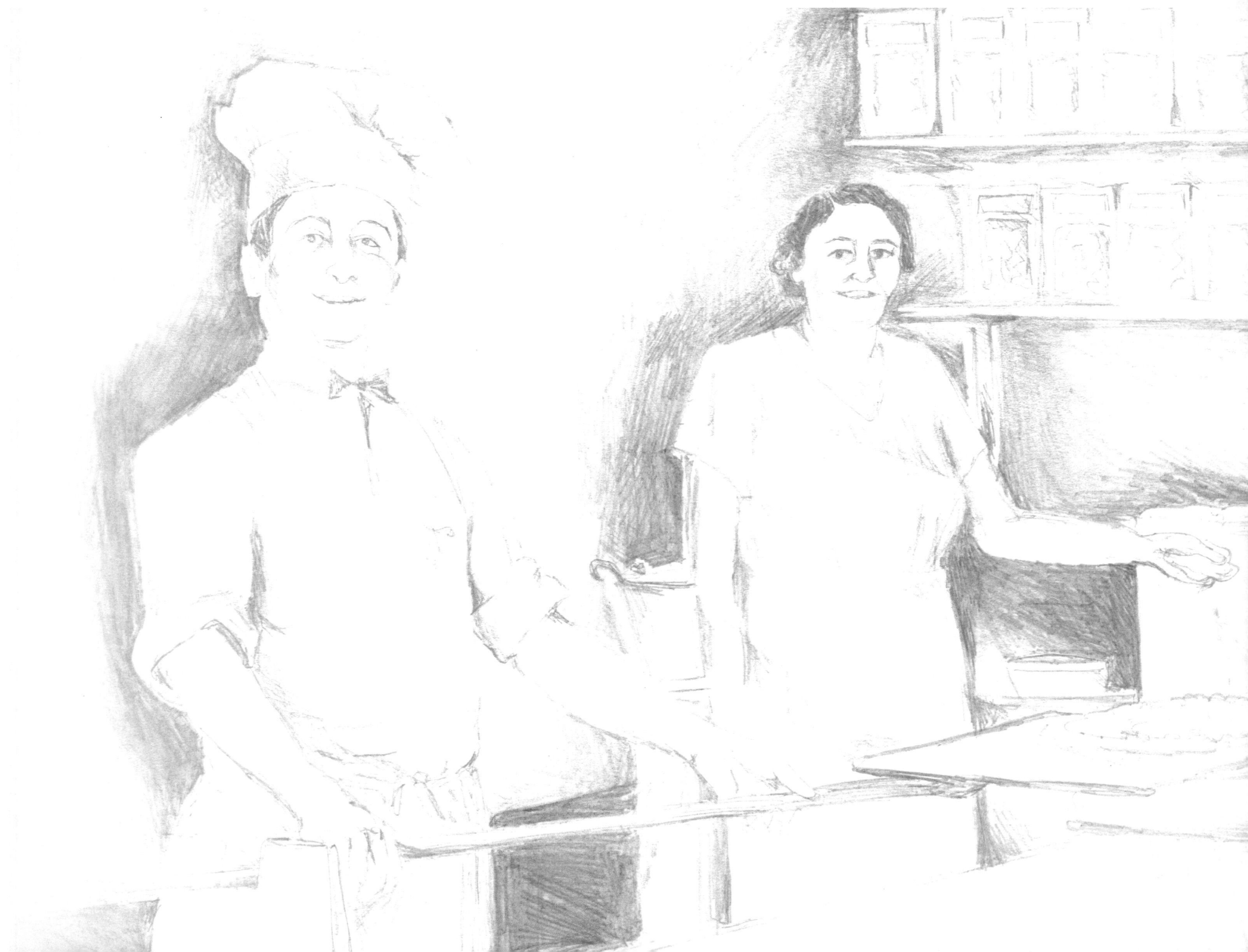

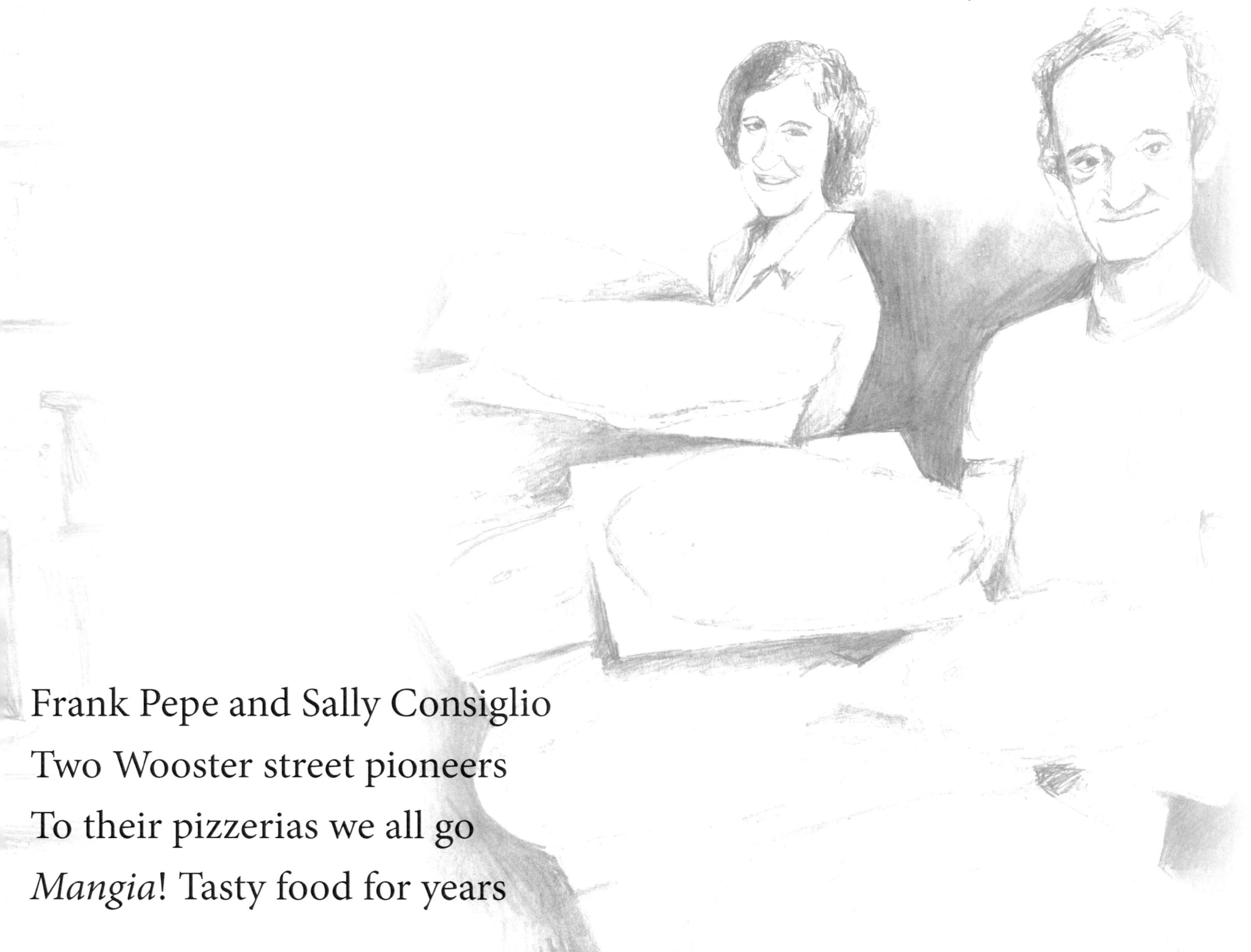

Frank Pepe and Sally Consiglio
Two Wooster street pioneers
To their pizzerias we all go
Mangia! Tasty food for years

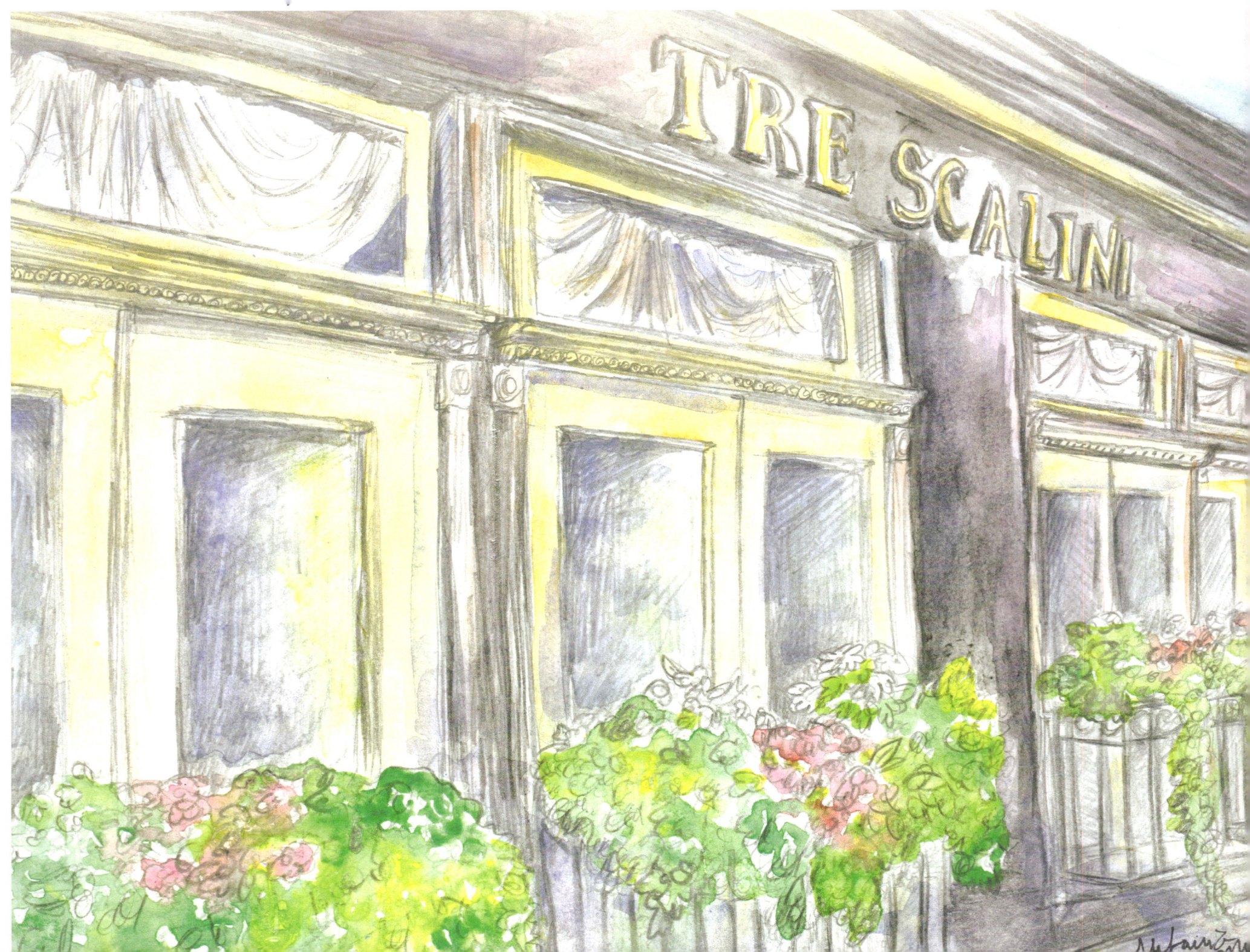

Tre Scalini, or "three little steps"
Has yummy Italian food too
Mangia pasta. It's simply the best.
They make it fresh for you.

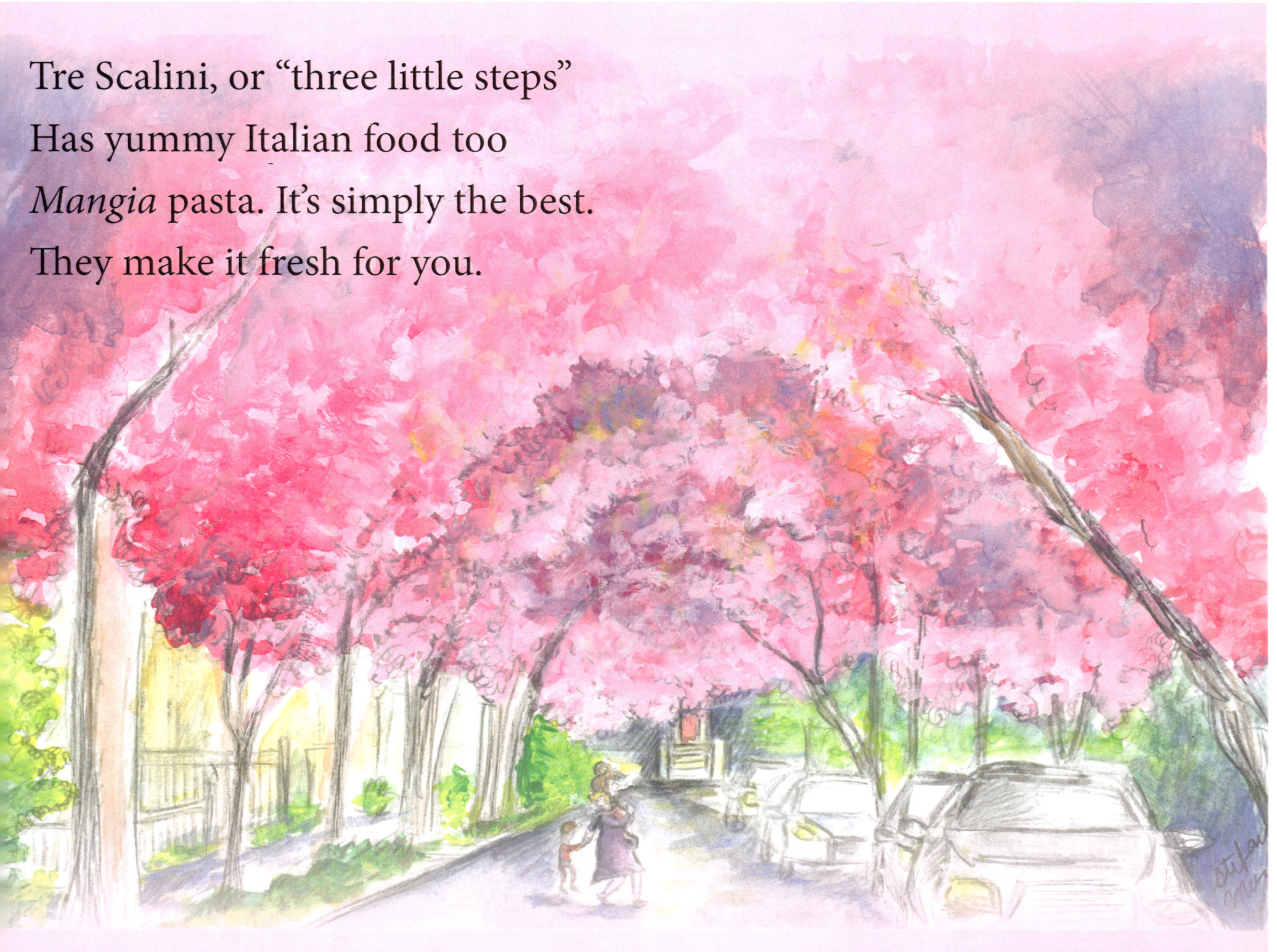

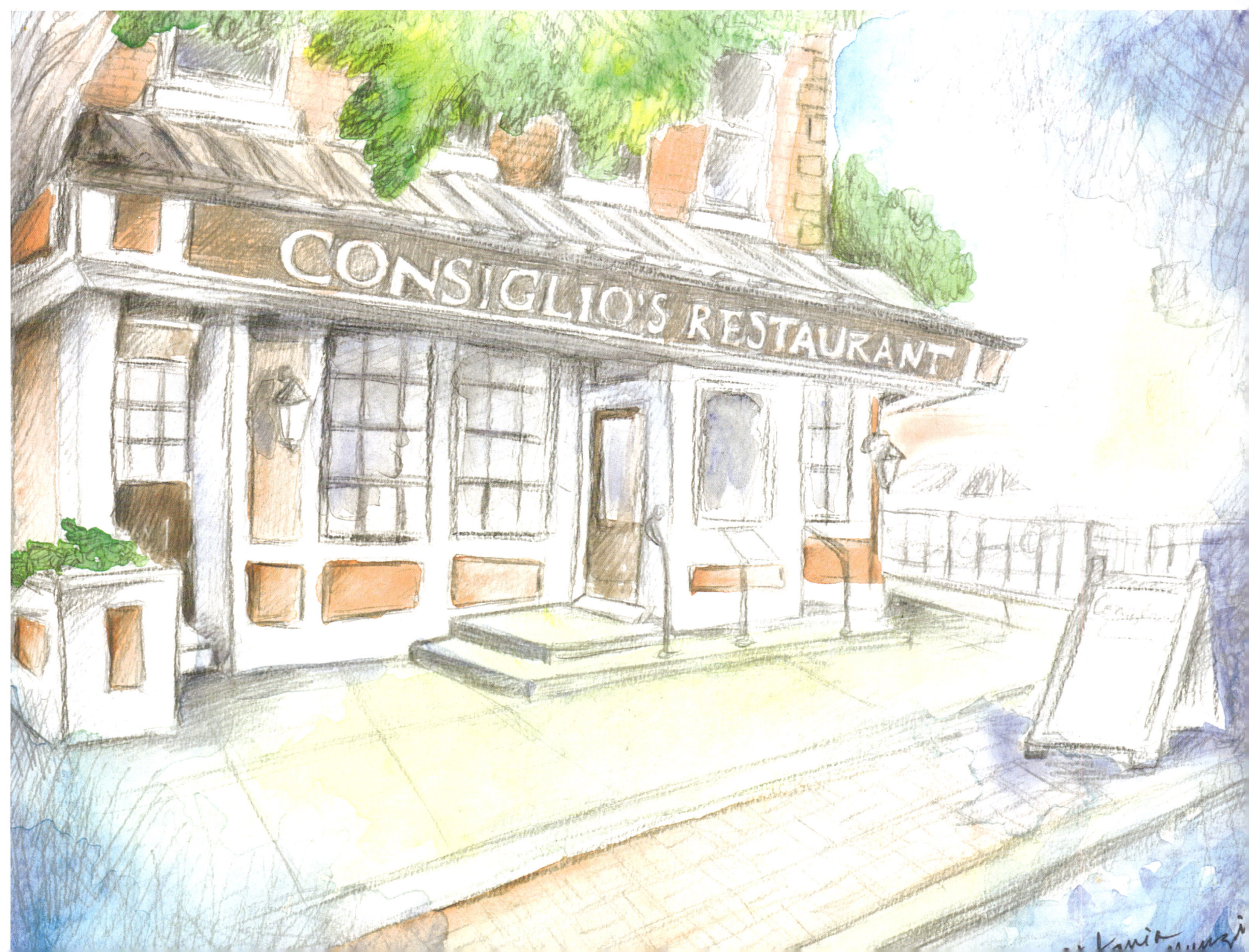

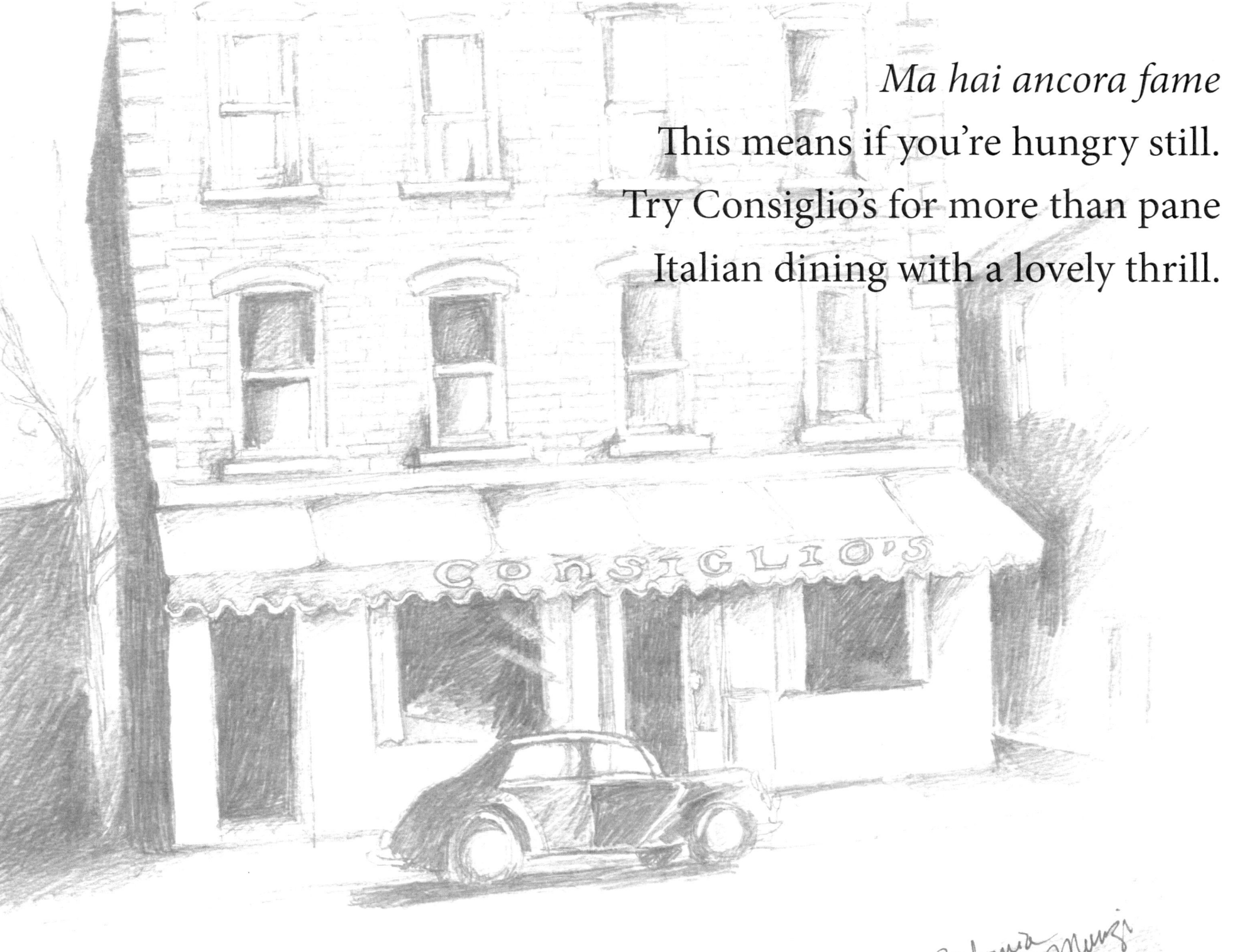

Ma hai ancora fame
This means if you're hungry still.
Try Consiglio's for more than pane
Italian dining with a lovely thrill.

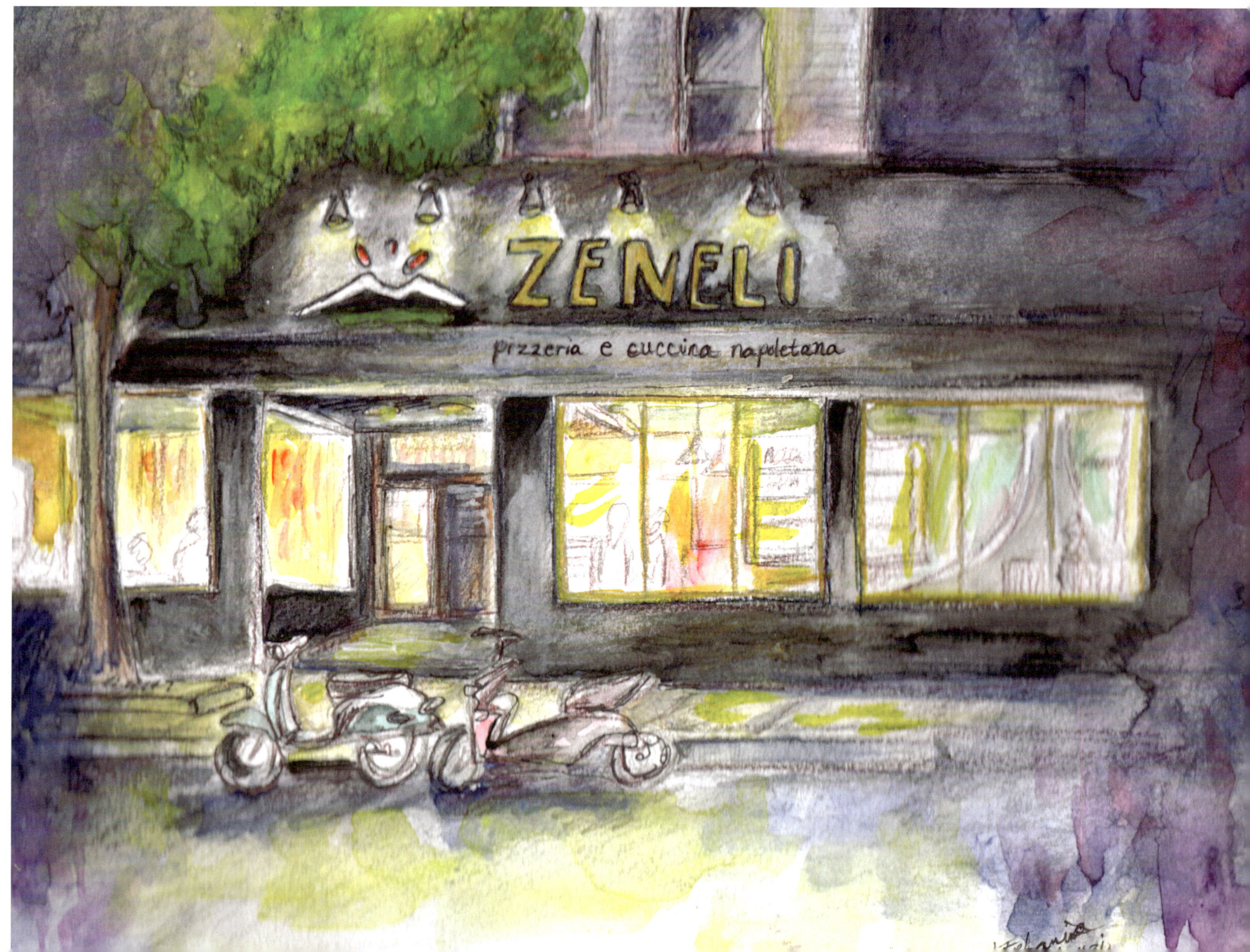

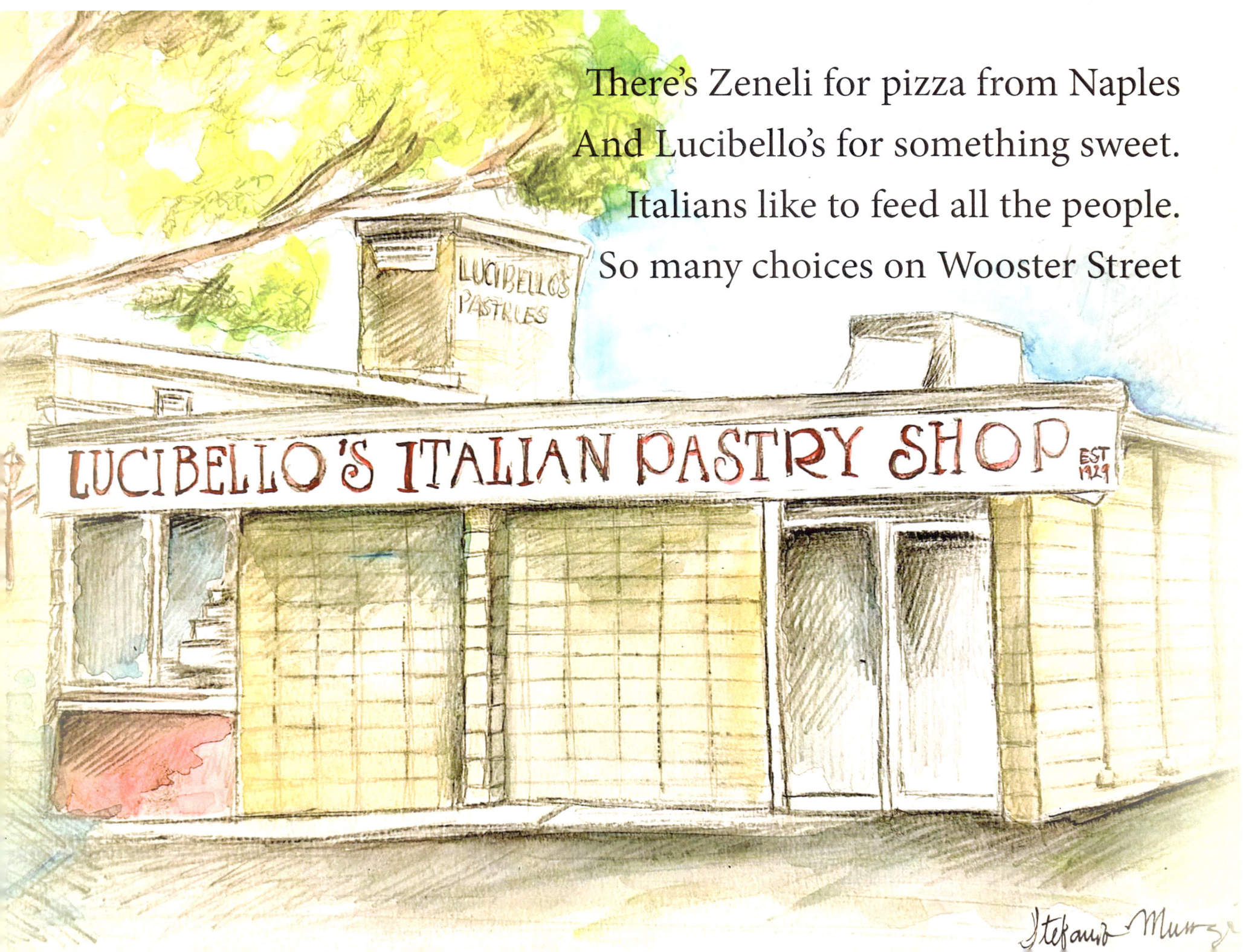

There's Zeneli for pizza from Naples
And Lucibello's for something sweet.
Italians like to feed all the people.
So many choices on Wooster Street

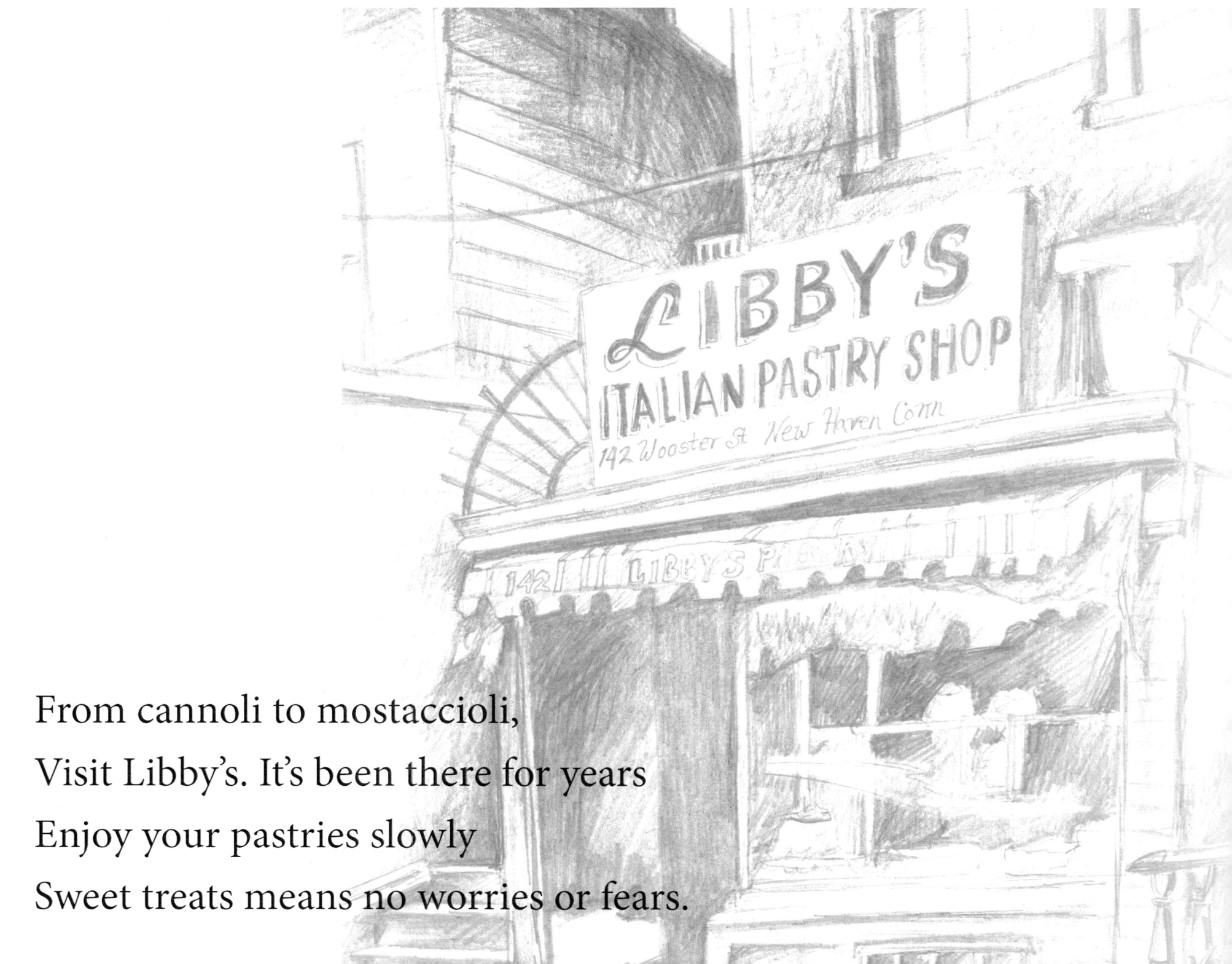

From cannoli to mostaccioli,
Visit Libby's. It's been there for years
Enjoy your pastries slowly
Sweet treats means no worries or fears.

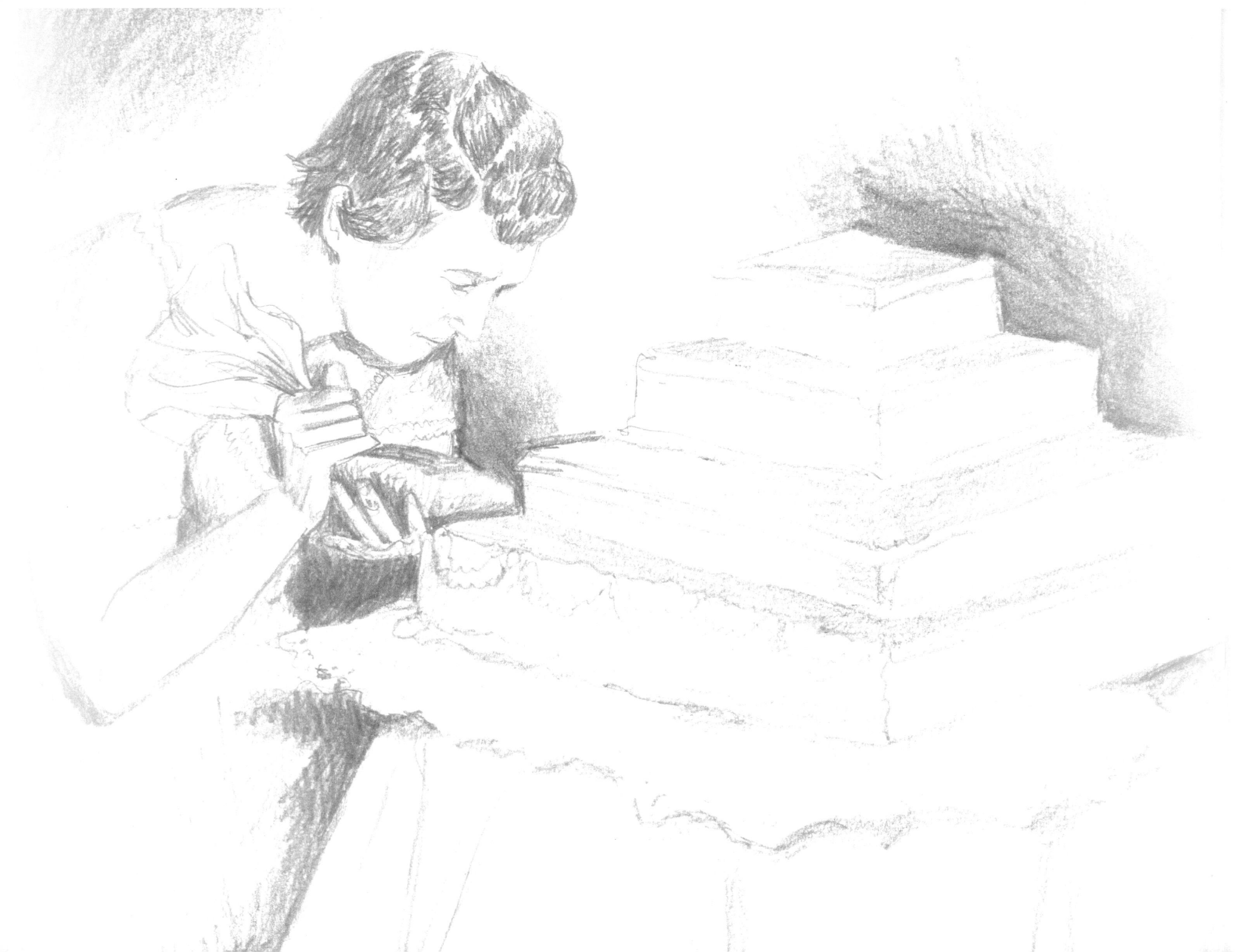

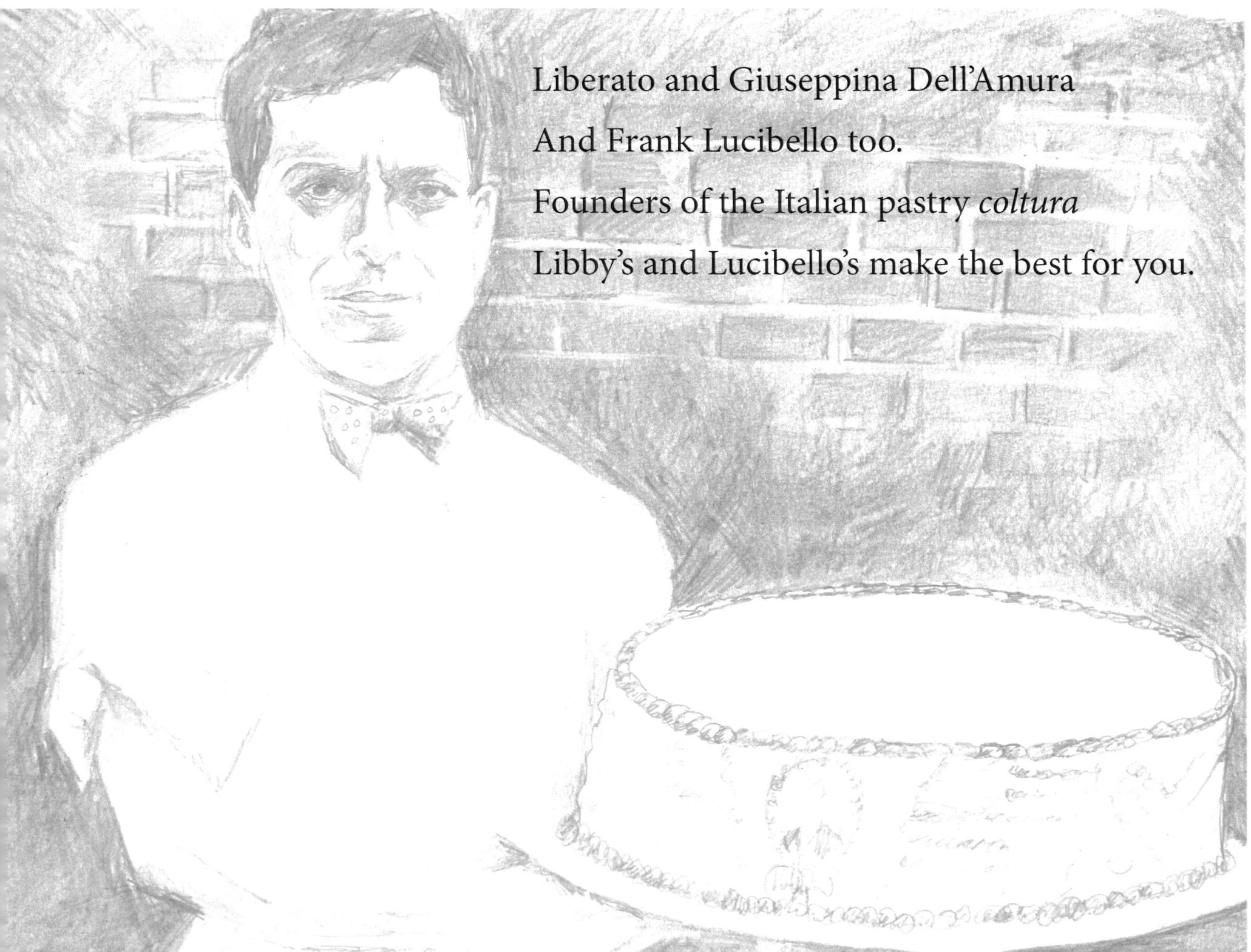

Liberato and Giuseppina Dell'Amura
And Frank Lucibello too.
Founders of the Italian pastry *coltura*
Libby's and Lucibello's make the best for you.

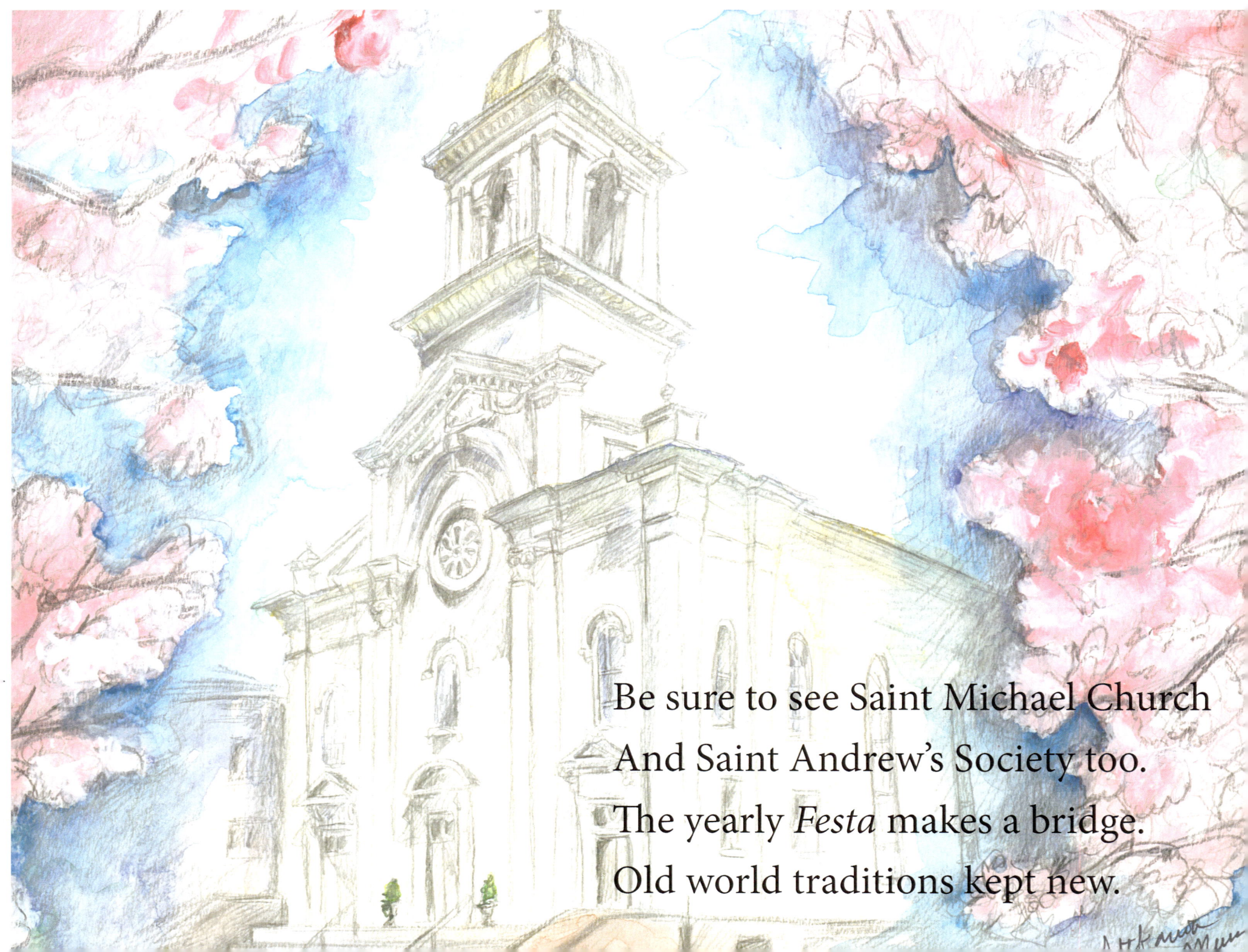

Be sure to see Saint Michael Church
And Saint Andrew's Society too.
The yearly *Festa* makes a bridge.
Old world traditions kept new.

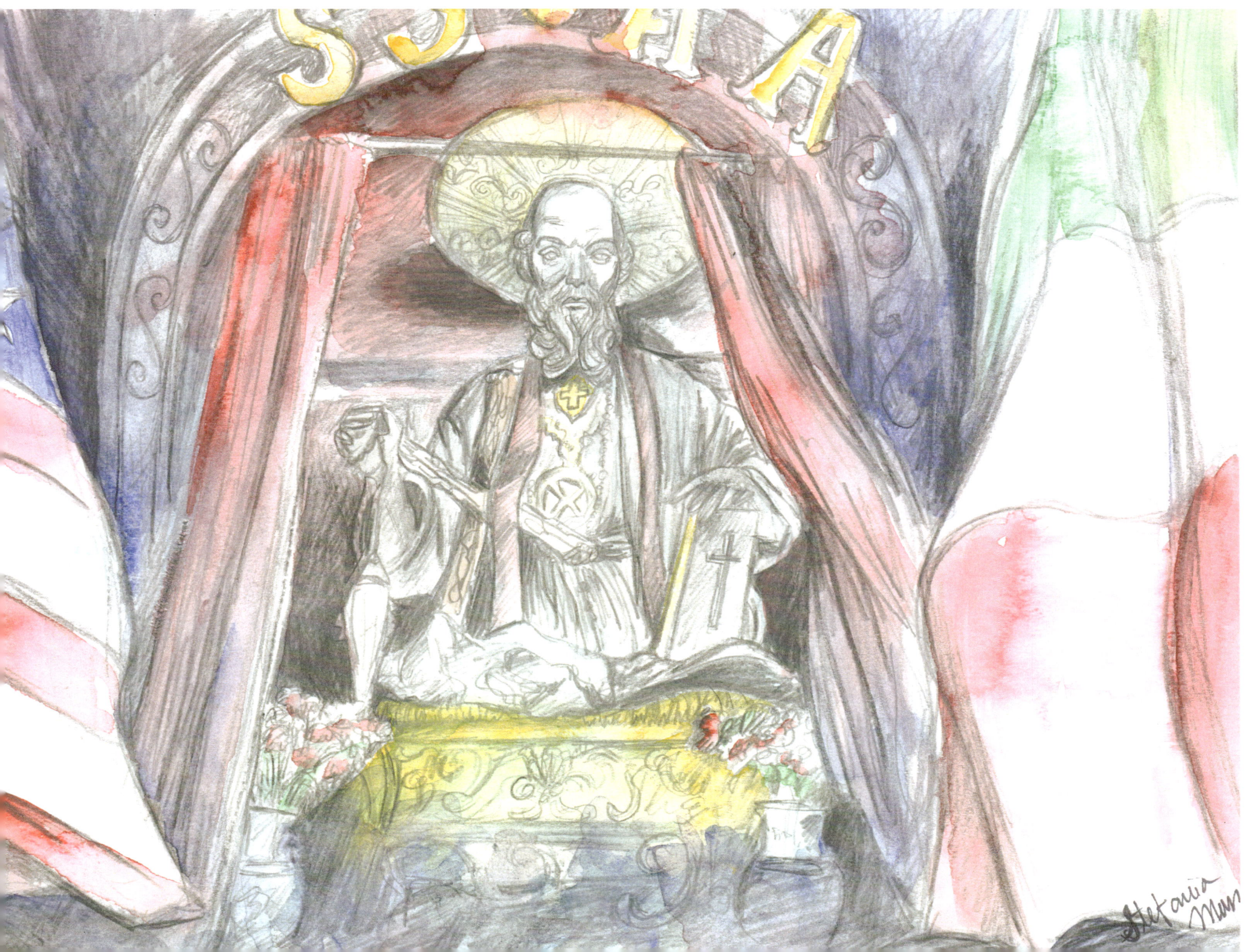

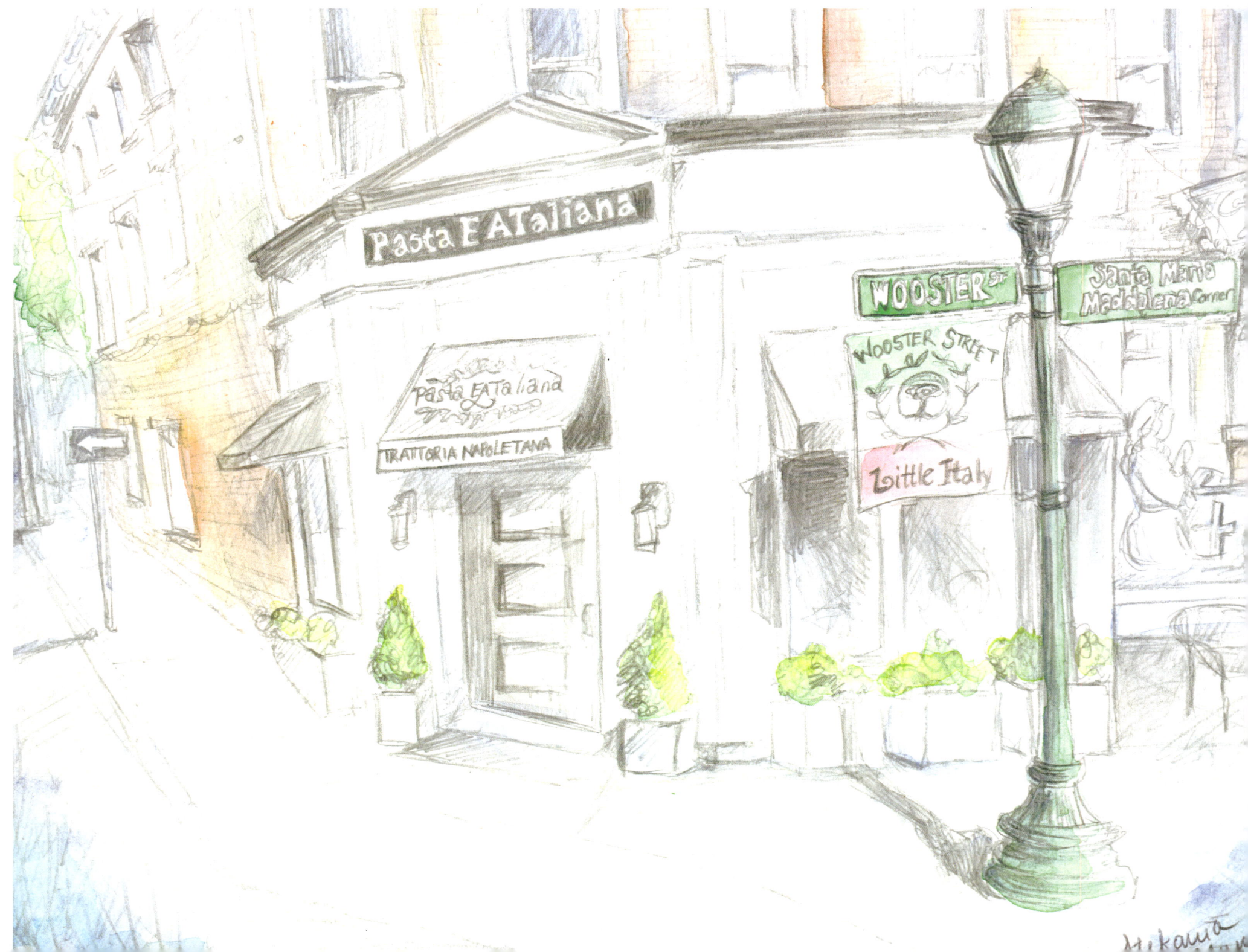

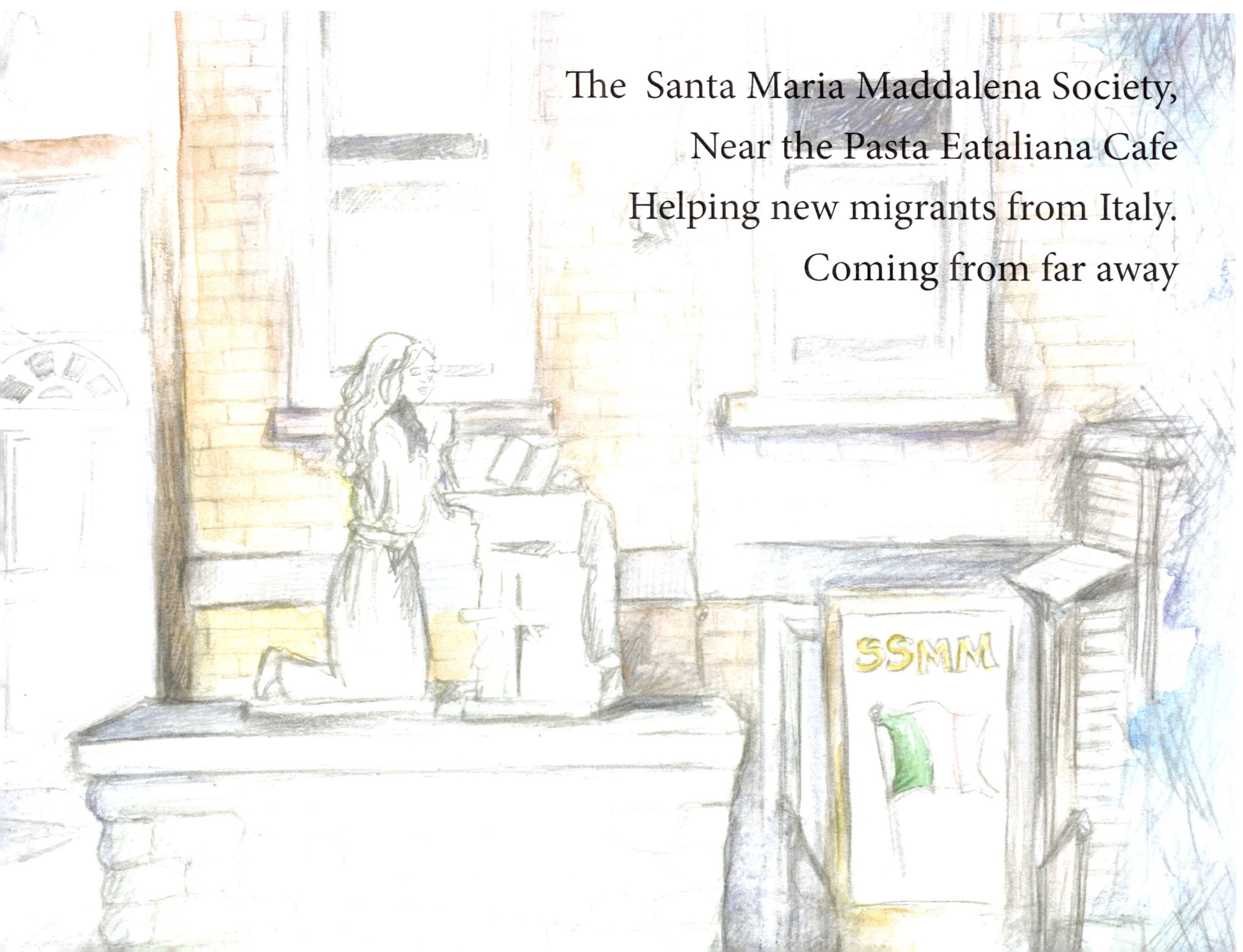

The Santa Maria Maddalena Society,
Near the Pasta Eataliana Cafe
Helping new migrants from Italy.
Coming from far away

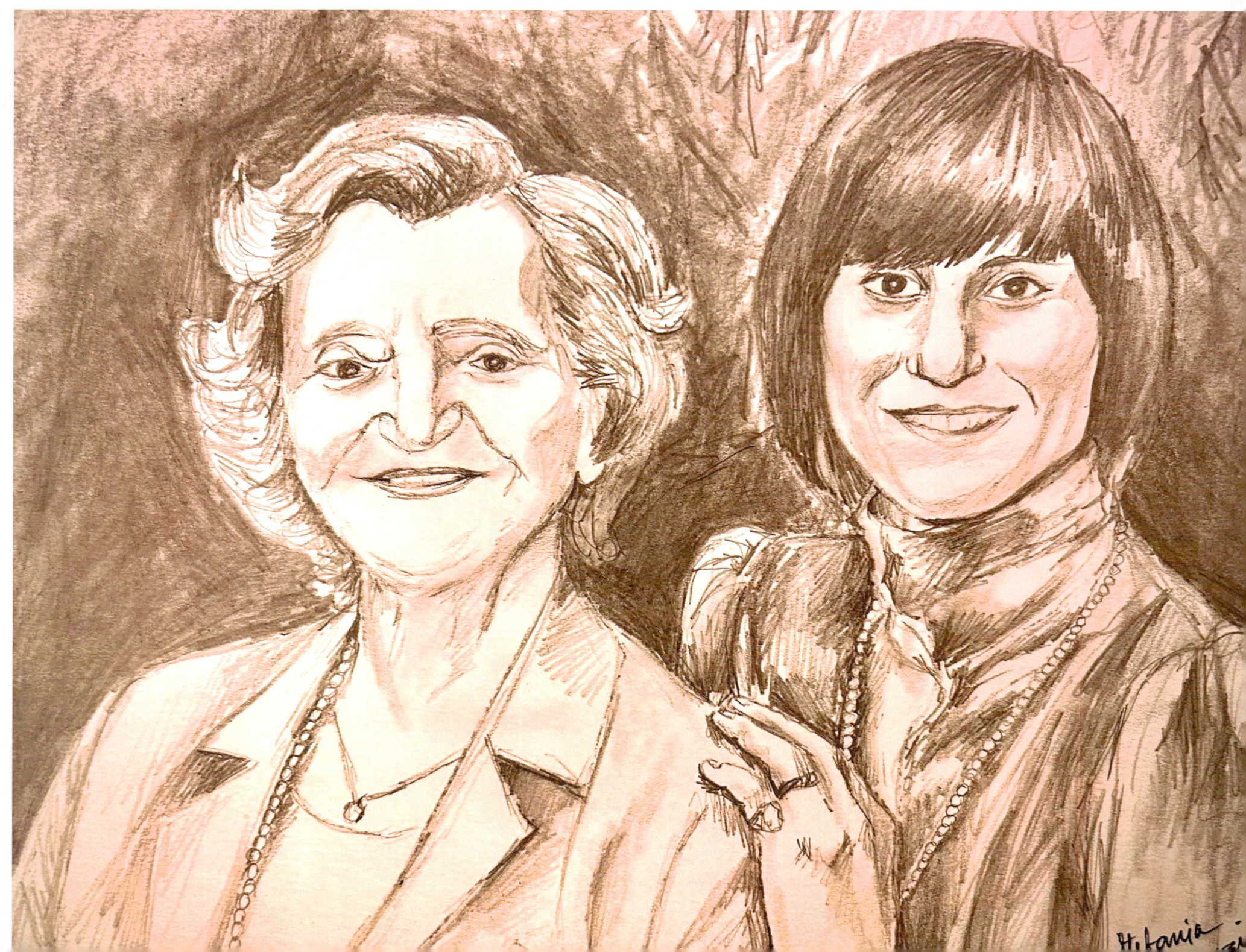

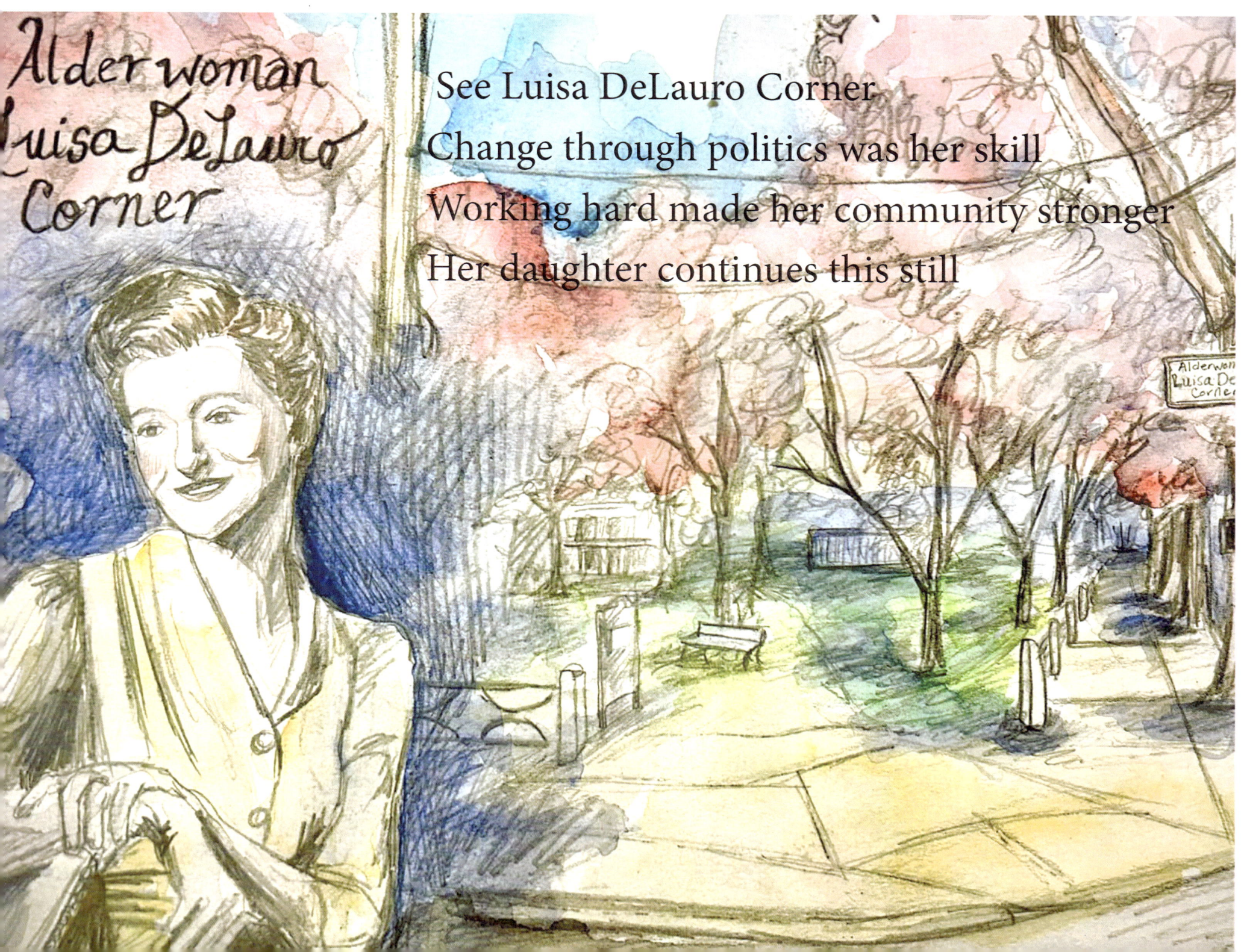

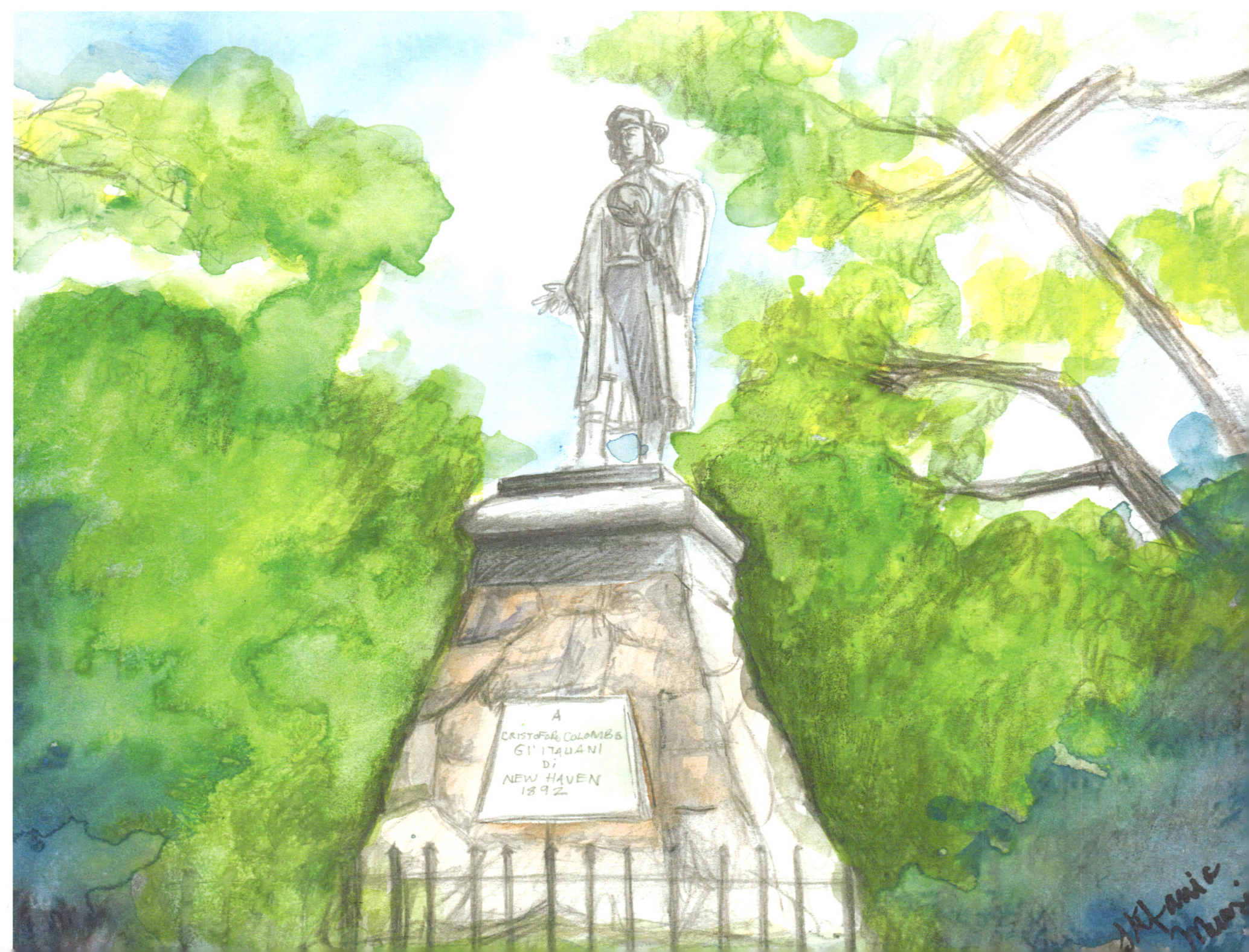

There are monuments old and new
In the center of Wooster Square.
This community prides its culture true.
La storia degli Italiani for all to share
"Indicando la via al futuro"
Towards our future we point the way.
More chances to flourish and grow,
But never forget those who paved the way.

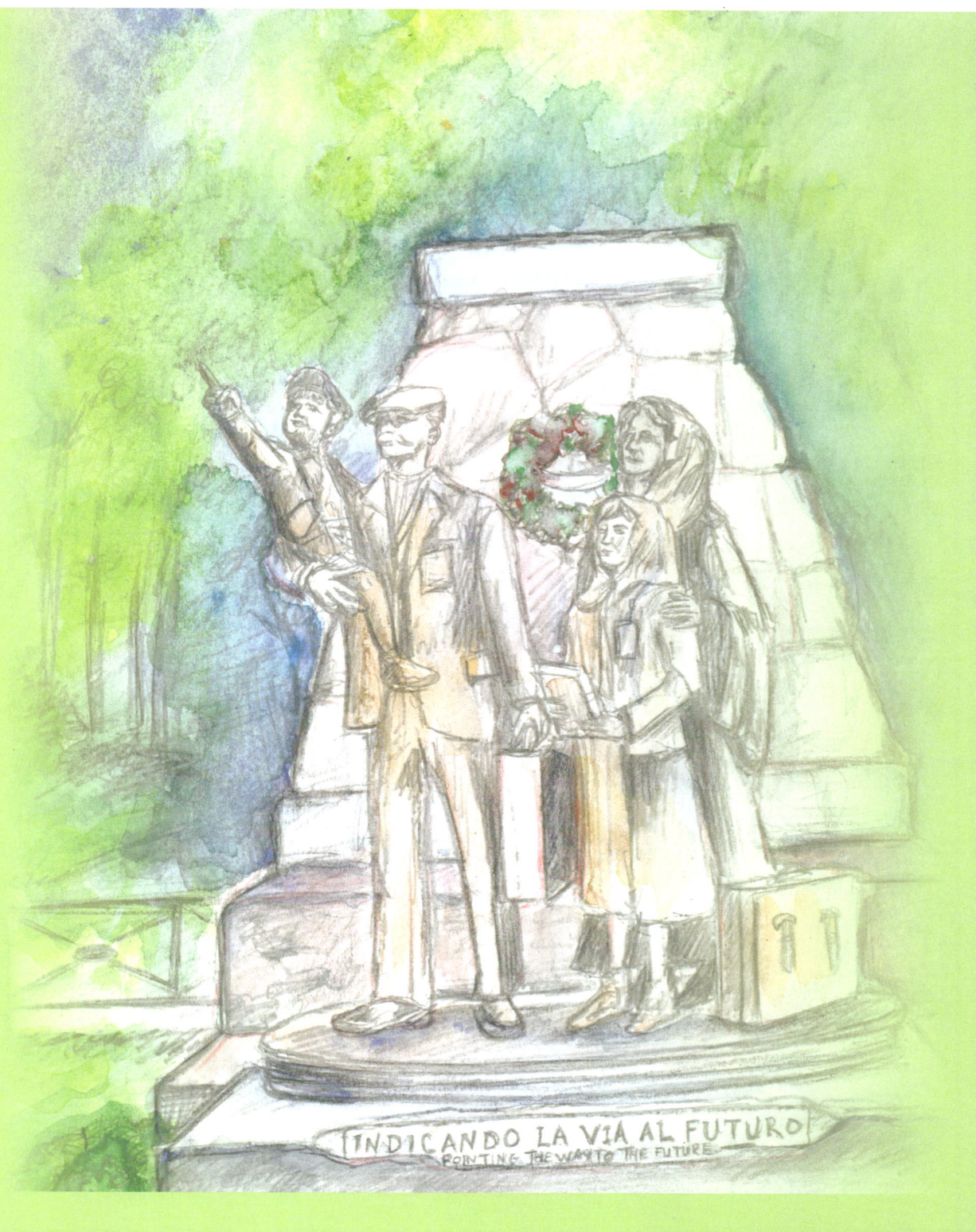

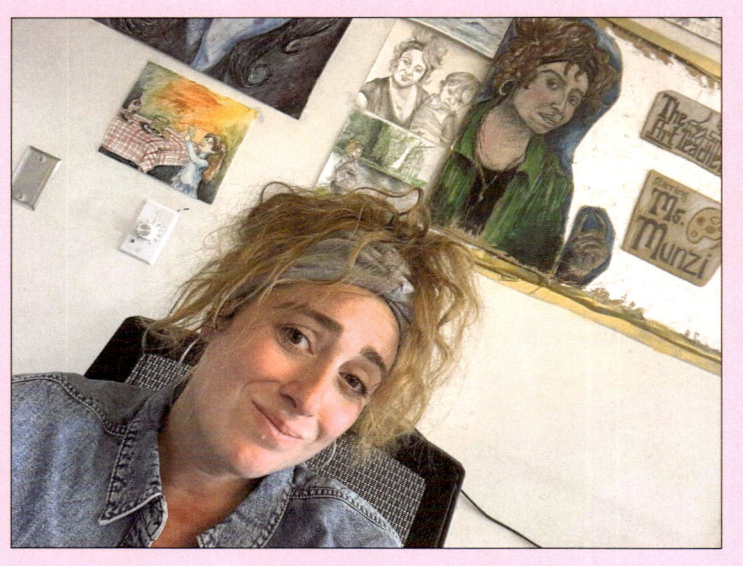 STEFANIA MUNZI is an artist and children's book author/illustrator based in Southern Connecticut. Her family originally came from Pratola Peligna in the Abruzzo region of Italy. She still stays in touch with her relatives there and her Italian roots are a large inspiration behind much of her work. It's no wonder she has a heartfelt connection to the iconic community of Italian Americans thriving in Wooster Square in New Haven.

As an artist, Munzi's style is based mostly in watercolor, as seen in the illustration work of *C'era Una Volta in Wooster Square*. In the past, her work has focused on the advocation of rights, services, and accommodations for special needs children, due to her oldest son being born with hearing loss.

Along with being an artist, illustrator, and author, Munzi is also a high school art teacher at the Hartford Magnet Trinity College Academy. Her classes primarily focus on painting and drawing skills. Art has always been a passion of hers that has driven her to create books to share with children and students from all walks of life.

Other work includes authoring and illustrating *Jojo's Tiny Ear* about her oldest son; illustration work for *The Check Minus*, a book depicting the town of Wallingford, Connecticut; and soon-to-come illustrations for Italian language children's books.

Learn more at https://www.stefaniamunzi.com

www.ingramcontent.com/pod-product-compliance
Lightning Source LLC
Chambersburg PA
CBRC090104160125
20423CB00035B/177